Tiny Talks

VOLUME 5:
I WILL FOLLOW GOD'S PLAN FOR ME

Janet Bernice

Tiny Talks

Volume 5
I Will Follow God's Plan For Me

**A year's worth of simple messages
that can be given during Primary
or Family Home Evening**

ISBN: 1-55517-815-4
e.1
Published by CFI
Imprint of Cedar Fort Inc.
www.cedarfort.com
Distributed by:

Cover design © 2004 by Lyle Mortimer
Illustrations © 2003 by Bob Bonham

Printed in the United States of America
10 9 8 7 6 5 4 3 2 1
Printed on acid-free paper

Library of Congress number: 2004096703

Tiny Talks

Volume 5: I Will Follow God's Plan For Me

A year's worth of simple messages
that can be given during Primary
or Family Home Evening

By Janet Bernice

Illustrated by Bob Bonham

CFI

Springville, Utah

Table of Contents

Introduction

As parents it is challenging to help create Primary talks that are simple enough for children to present and understand, while keeping sharing time interesting. This fifth volume of *Tiny Talks* will help children, and adults alike, develop primary or family home evening talks. It is also a great way to promote quality time for families as parents and children work together to prepare for these very special and important events.

The following editions are also available:

Volume 1 is linked to the 2002 Primary theme of **Temples** and their importance.

Volume 2 is **The Savior**, written to help Primary children understand the mission of Jesus Christ and grow closer to him.

Volume 3 focuses on the 2003 Primary theme of **The Church of Jesus Christ** and the restored gospel.

Volume 4 is tied to the 2004 Primary theme **My Family Can Be Forever.** Many stories in this volume come from the childhood experiences of the modern prophets.

Volume 5 follows the 2005 Primary theme *I Will Follow God's Plan for Me*.

Along with the presentation text are suggestions for pictures. It is always fun for a child to use a visual aid when presenting his part of Family Home Evening or Primary sharing time. The pictures listed come from the Primary-approved Gospel Art Picture Kit (GAPK). This package of pictures is available from the Church Distribution Center or might also be found in the meetinghouse library. There are other pictures as well, in the meetinghouse library that can be substituted.

When your child (or grandchild, in my case) has completed his talk, he might end with a short testimony and close by saying, "In the name of Jesus Christ, amen."

It is our wish at Cedar Fort, Inc. that this new volume of *Tiny Talks* will prove informative, enjoyable, and helpful as you teach your children the gospel, whatever your role may be in their lives. Enjoy!

~ Janet Bernice ~

Chapter 1:

Heavenly Father presented a plan for us to become like Him

Scripture:

For behold, this is my work and my glory—to bring to pass the immortality and eternal life of man. (Moses: 1:39)

Visual Aid:
GAPK # 100
Creation - Living Creatures

Heavenly Father presented His plan and we all shouted for joy.

Our Heavenly Father loves us so much that he provided a plan for us to help us grow and progress. We learned about this wonderful plan at a meeting called the Grand Council in Heaven, before we were born. We were so excited about it that we all shouted for joy. This is the plan of salvation.

Jesus supported the plan and said he would also come to earth and help us by setting a perfect example, teaching us, and paying for our sins if we would try hard to do what is right. We were all very excited by this idea and voted for Heavenly Father's plan.

Lucifer tried to change the plan. He wanted to do things his way by forcing all of us to do what's right. But Heavenly Father's plan was to let us choose for ourselves, and He hoped we would choose to follow Jesus.

Lucifer and his followers were removed from heaven and will never be allowed to have bodies. We were sad, but knew that Heavenly Father's plan would make us happy and we could live with Him again someday.

Heavenly Father provided a Savior.

Our Heavenly Father knew that when we came to earth, we would make mistakes. Sometimes we would need help to be forgiven for those mistakes when they are more serious and called sins. So he provided a Savior, Jesus Christ, to help us repent and be forgiven.

What the Savior did for us is called the Atonement. Jesus went to a garden and prayed for us. He felt the weight of all the sins of all the people who would ever live on earth, including your sins and mine. He paid the price and was then crucified for us because he loves us more than we can know.

The Savior set a perfect example for us. He was always serving others. He healed the sick, he taught the gospel, and he was kind and forgiving. He was even baptized to show us how important it is for us to do the same.

If we want to be happy and return home to be with the Savior, Heavenly Father, and our loved ones, we must try to do like Jesus did—help others, be kind to everyone (especially parents, and brothers and sisters), and ask forgiveness when mistakes or sins are committed.

Scripture

Behold, I am he who was prepared from the foundation of the world to redeem my people.
Behold, I am Jesus Christ.
(Ether 3:14)

Visual Aid:
GAPK # 239
The Resurrected Jesus Christ

The earth was created as part of the Plan.

As part of Heavenly Father's plan, this beautiful earth was created. Heavenly Father and Jesus worked together and it took six days for this to happen. The scriptures say everything on the earth existed in heaven first in a spiritual way, just like us.

When the earth was being formed, it was important that first there be day-time and night-time; and later, Father also gave us the sun, moon, and stars. Next came dry land and all the water was divided into seas. Then came plants and trees, and fruits, herbs, and vegetables. And finally, all the animals came—in the sea, in the air, and every living creature on the ground.

Then God made man in his own image, both male and female. They were called Adam and Eve and they were in charge of all the earth and took care of all the animals and plants. They got to name the animals and keep the garden of Eden beautiful.

Heavenly Father saw all He made and blessed it. Then he rested on the seventh day when all his work was done and said this is very good.

Scripture:

In the beginning God created the heaven and the earth.
(Genesis 1:1)

Visual Aid:
GAPK # 600
The World

Adam and Eve fulfilled their part of Heavenly Father's plan

Adam and Eve lived in the Garden of Eden and Heavenly Father visited them. He taught them many things—how to take care of the garden and to be kind, and take care of all the animals.

Heavenly Father also taught Adam and Eve that they should not eat the fruit of a tree called the Tree of Knowledge of Good and Evil. If they disobeyed, they would have to leave the garden.

Satan, also known as Lucifer, came into the garden and tempted Adam and Eve. They *did* eat the fruit, so Heavenly Father told them they had to go out into the world as we know it now. He wouldn't be able to come down and visit them anymore, but if they prayed, Heavenly Father would listen and answer their prayers.

Adam and Eve were sad about leaving the garden, but then they began to have children and taught their children about the plan of salvation. This was all part of God's plan so we could come to earth, too. We call Adam and Eve our first parents.

Scripture

So God created man in his own image, in the image of God created he him; male and female created he them.
(Genesis 1:27)

Visual Aid:
GAPK # 101
Adam and Eve

Chapter 2:

I am a Child of God

I came to earth to receive a body and be tested.

Scripture:

For behold, this life is the time for men to prepare to meet God; yea, behold the day of this life is the day for men to perform their labors.
(Alma 34:32)

Visual Aid:
Bring own picture of newborn or small baby.

Part of our Heavenly Father's plan was for each of us to receive a body when we came to earth. Without a physical body, we cannot progress or learn to be obedient and choose the right.

But first, we were created as spirit children of a Heavenly Father and Mother. All the people on earth are our brothers and sisters, too, and chose to follow God's plan during the Great Council in Heaven. This earned us the right to come to earth and get these precious bodies.

We all began life by being born. Then we grew into a child, and some day we will be an adult. Our mothers and fathers guide us and teach us correct principles and how to keep the commandments.

Our bodies are made of flesh and bone, just like our heavenly parents, who have resurrected bodies of flesh and bone. If we keep the commandments, help each other, and try to be more like Jesus every day, we will be able to live with our heavenly parents again and have resurrected bodies that will be perfect in every way.

Heavenly Father has given me agency, and I am accountable for my choices.

There are some things all people on earth have in common. We are all born and we all will die some day. Another important gift, maybe the most important one, is agency. This great gift from God to all his children is part of the plan of salvation. The scriptures say:

"And the Messiah cometh in the fulness of time, that he may redeem the children of men from the fall. And because they are redeemed from the fall they have become free forever, knowing good from evil, to act for themselves. (2 Nephi 2:26.)

This means I'm the only person who can choose good or bad for myself and Heavenly Father holds me responsible—or accountable—for what I choose. If I want to do only what *I* think is fun or good without doing what I know is right, I am following my own will and not Heavenly Father's. But if I try to remember the commandments and do the things my teachers and parents teach me, I can make the right choices and be happy.

Scripture

Wherefore, men are free according to the flesh . . . and they are free to choose liberty and eternal life . . . or to choose captivity and death.
(2 Nephi:2:27)

Visual Aid:
GAPK # 615
Serving One Another

I can pray to Heavenly Father and receive answers to my prayers.

Scripture:

But behold, I say unto you that ye must pray always, and not faint.
(2 Nephi 32:9)

Visual Aid:
GAPK # 605
Young Boy Praying

One of the best ways to know what is right or wrong is to pray. Prayer is the way we talk to Heavenly Father.

When you talk to someone, you usually say their name first. So when you pray to Father in Heaven, you call his name—Dear Father in Heaven or Heavenly Father.

Second, count your blessings and tell Father all the things you are thankful for—your food, your family, the gospel, the prophet. Sometimes saying thanks for blessings is all a person wants to do in a prayer. This makes Heavenly Father very happy. Other times, we have special needs. We can ask for help to know what is right, we can ask for someone to be healed who is sick, or we can even ask for Heavenly Father to help a mom or dad come home safe from a trip.

When you are done talking to Heavenly Father, be very still for a little while and see if you can feel his answer in your heart or mind. Then close your prayer by saying, "in the name of Jesus Christ, Amen." Heavenly Father is always available anytime to hear our prayers.

I show my love for Heavenly Father by keeping the commandments and respecting his creations.

Heavenly Father showed his love for us in many ways—He gave us the right to choose for ourselves, He created a beautiful world where we can live with our families and be surrounded by trees, flowers, bird song, and colorful scenery, and we are born into this world and receive a body to help us learn to obey.

When we obey Heavenly Father and keep his commandments, we show him how grateful we are for all our blessings. One way to obey is by showing respect for all the things He created.

We know animals were so important they were saved by Noah. When a pet is cared for or we help an animal in any way, it makes Heavenly Father happy. When we pick up litter and are careful not to step on flowers or hurt trees, we also show our love to Father in Heaven. I can show my love for Heavenly Father by being careful when I am in nature and show respect for all living things.

Scripture

If ye love me, keep my commandments. (John 14:15)

Visual Aid:
GAPK # 100 or 103
Animals/Creation
Animals and Noah's Ark

Chapter 3:

Jesus Christ came to earth and is our Savior

Jesus Christ organized His Church when he lived on earth.

Scripture:

And when he had called unto him his twelve disciples, he gave them power against unclean spirits, to cast them out, and to heal all manner of sickness. (Matthew 10:1)

The Savior knew it was very important to have people to help lead and teach the true gospel, so he organized his Church among his faithful followers, with apostles, prophets, and other teachers. He sent these good disciples into all the world to teach without using force, but out of kindness and love for their fellows.

The Lord set up his program of organization, taught all that Heavenly Father wanted him to teach, and assigned his followers to go and do the same. His Church was set up by a divine plan.

The Lord knew his small church could not last long against the wickedness that would come, but he left some very strong apostles to guide and build the kingdom. These were good men who had kind hearts and wanted to do what was right—Peter, James, Luke, and John were some of these men. And today, we have the words of Jesus because they wrote down the things Jesus said and did. Their writings are now called the Holy Bible.

Visual Aid:
GAPK # 211
Christ Ordaining the Apostles

Jesus Christ taught the gospel and set the example by how He lived.

From the time he was a young boy, Jesus taught the gospel by the things he did, by setting a good example. He helped his father Joseph, who was a carpenter, and he taught men the gospel in the temple.

When Jesus was thirty, he started teaching the gospel in many different towns. He traveled first to his cousin John who was baptizing people in the Jordan River. Jesus was baptized by immersion by John, even though he was perfect, to set the example for us.

Jesus loved little children and always talked with them. He also taught people how to be happy by keeping the commandments. He healed the sick and blind, and he kept the Sabbath day holy.

Jesus had a meal called the Last Supper. He washed the feet of his apostles, and gave the first sacrament, telling his followers that the sacrament was to remember him. We still take the sacrament each week to remember Jesus and his example, and to try harder to repent and follow Him every day.

Scripture

Let your light so shine before men, that they may see your good works, and glorify your Father which is in heaven.
(Matthew 5:16)

Visual Aid:
GAPK # 226
Jesus Washing the Apostles' Feet

Jesus paid for my sins and I can repent and live with Him and Heavenly Father again.

Scripture:

For as in Adam all die, even so in Christ shall all be made alive.
(1 Corinthians 15:22)

Jesus paid for our sins by suffering in the Garden of Gethsemane. He asked Heavenly Father to bless him because he could feel the weight of all the sins of the people who would ever live on earth—even yours and mine. An angel then came to comfort Jesus. Later that same evening, some Roman soldiers came and took him to be crucified.

As members of his true Church, we owe everything to the Savior for what he did for us. We show our love for Him by trying to be like Him—being kind to others, helping whenever we can, and forgiving people when they hurt our feelings.

The scriptures teach us that we can live with Jesus again someday. To do this, we must keep the command-ments and try every day to do a little better. If we repent when we make mistakes, Heavenly Father will bless us and we are promised that we can live with our families in the Celestial Kingdom if we will be faithful and not ever give up trying to be good.

Visual Aid:
GAPK # 234
Jesus Shows His Wounds

The Savior die and was resurrected, and now all Heavenly Father's children will be resurrected, too.

After Jesus died on the cross, some of his friends came and buried him in a tomb in a garden. On the third day after his burial, two angels rolled away the stone in front of his tomb. Then his friend, Mary Magdalene, came to visit the tomb, but she was very sad to see the stone had been moved and that the Savior's body was gone.

Then a man came that Mary thought was the gardener. She asked him what he had done with the Savior's body, but he spoke to her and said, "Mary." She realized it was Jesus because she recognized his voice. He was resurrected! His body and spirit were together again in perfect form.

Because Jesus was resurrected, all people who have lived or who will ever live on this earth, will also be resurrected. Because of the resurrection, we do not have to fear dying, because we know our bodies and spirits will come back together again, as well as those of people we love who have already gone to heaven.

Scripture

I am the resurrection and the life: he that believeth in me, though he were dead, yet shall he live.
(John 11:25)

Visual Aid:
GAPK # 239
The Resurrected Jesus Christ

17

Chapter 4:
I will follow Heavenly Father's plan for me and do my part to have an eternal family

Heavenly Father planned for me to come to a family.

Scripture:

I Nephi, having been born of goodly parents, therefore I was taught somewhat in all the learning of my father.
(1 Nephi 1:1)

Visual Aid:
GAPK # 606 - Family prayer

Families are at the center of our Heavenly Father's plan. Adam and Eve were the first parents and had children when they left the Garden of Eden. They taught their children about Heavenly Father's plan.

Families are so important, that President Hinckley, our prophet, presented "The Family: A Proclamation to the World". This is some of what it says:

"'Children are an heritage of the Lord' (Psalms 127:3). Parents have a sacred duty to rear their children in love and righteousness, to provide for their physical and spiritual needs, to teach them to love and serve one another, to observe the commandments of God and to be law-abiding citizens wherever they live."

Heavenly Father loves his children and he will not leave us to guess about what matters most in this life. He has given us family to teach, guide and protect us. No matter who your family is—mother and father, brothers, sisters, or grandparents, you can learn and grow, serve one another, love and be loved.

I can learn the gospel in my home.

Family is the best place to learn how to be more like the Savior. Before we came to earth, we were sons and daughters in our heavenly home with parents who knew and loved us. We learned about the gospel, about living good lives, and about doing what is right. Then we were born to an earthly home to a family where we could continue to learn and grow.

We can become like our Heavenly Father and enjoy the kind of life He lives only by keeping the commandments. Therefore, we must know what those rules or commandments are.

Jesus taught us to search and study the scriptures. Families can study the scriptures together every day. Fathers should gather their families together at a regular time each day to read and each family member who *can* read should take a turn to read. A family member may offer a prayer before the scripture reading and ask Heavenly Father to bless each one to understand what is being read. Learning about the gospel together helps families stay close and find happiness.

Scripture

Train up a child in the way he should go, and when he is old, he will not depart from it.
(Proverbs 22:6)

Visual Aid:
GAPK # 616
Family Togetherness

I will honor my parents and do my part to strengthen my family.

Scripture:

Children, obey your parents in the Lord: for this is right. Honour thy father and mother; (which is the first commandment with promise;) That it may be well with thee, and thou mayest live long on the earth.
(Ephesians 6:1-3)

Visual Aid:
GAPK # 616
Serving One Another

The Lord wants us to have joy and happiness in our lives. To help us, he has provided important guides, such as the scriptures, a living prophet, other Church leaders, and the Holy Spirit. All these guides can help us understand and keep the commandments. Being obedient will bring joy to us and our families.

Our homes are the best places to learn to be like Jesus. If someone asks us to take out the garbage or water the plants, we can do our share and remember that when we obey, we are also doing what Heavenly Father wants us to. We feel good when we do what is right.

Sometimes it is hard to be nice to a brother or sister. Sometimes we get angry or get our feelings hurt. This is when we can have faith in Heavenly Father and pray to Him. We can ask Him to help us understand our family members and be forgiving and be kind. When we keep trying to do the things we are taught through the Holy Spirit, we do our part to strengthen our family and make home a happy and safe place.

My family can be together forever through the blessings of the temple.

The prophet Elijah was a good man who lived many years before Jesus was born. He loved Heavenly Father very much and Heavenly Father was very pleased with Elijah. He gave him a special duty to provide the sealing power in temples.

On April 3, 1836, Elijah visited Joseph Smith and gave him the keys to this sealing power. Now families could be sealed together—husbands to wives and children to parents. With these keys and priesthood authority returned to earth, all who are worthy to receive the blessings of eternal families can go to the temple.

"Yea the hearts of thousands and tens of thousands shall greatly rejoice in consequence of the blessings which shall be poured out . . . " (D&C 110:9)

Families can be sealed in any of the temples around the world, and they can do the work for their deceased ancestors, too. It is a wonderful promise to be together forever if we try to do what is right and keep the commandments.

Scripture

The prophet Elijah was to plant in the hearts of the children the promises made to their fathers, . . . the great work to be done in the temples of the Lord in the dispensation of the fulness of times, for the redemption of the dead and the sealing of the children to their parents.
(D&C 138: 47-48)

Visual Aid:
GAPK # 505
Washington Temple

Chapter 5:

Jesus Christ restored His Church in the latter days

Authority and truth were lost during the Great Apostasy, then Joseph Smith had the First Vision.

When Jesus began to teach the gospel in his day, he also organized his Church among his faithful followers, with apostles, prophets, and teachers. But the Lord knew his small church could not last long against the wickedness which was to come, because Satan wanted men to be unhappy and not follow the Savior. Over time, the true church was lost and the priesthood—the power of God— was taken from the earth. This was called the Great Apostasy.

In 1820, a young man of fourteen named Joseph Smith wanted to know which church was right to join. He went to a grove of trees near his father's farm and prayed with all his heart to know the truth. Heavenly Father and the Savior appeared to him and told him none of the churches were true and if he would be faithful, he could help restore the Church just as it was in Christ's day. This is called the Restoration. Today we have the priesthood again and all the blessings of the church as it was in Jesus' day because of one boy's prayer.

Joseph Smith translated the Book of Mormon.

Joseph Smith was raised on a farm in New York and he was only twenty-four when he finished translating the golden plates into the Book of Mormon. In order to translate these books, Joseph used special stones called Seers, or the Urim and Thummin, provided by the Lord.

While Joseph was translating, he also had to take care of his wife and family, plant and harvest crops, chop wood, haul water, and care for animals.

Many times while Joseph was translating, mobs tried to kill him and steal the plates, so he had to hide the ancient records and move them from place to place.

Joseph had no telephone, no computer, or copy machine—not even electric light. He changed words written in Egyptian into English, and he had only gone to school through the third grade. So how did Joseph translate? Oliver Cowdery, his main helper, said, "the Prophet Joseph Smith . . . translated [the Book of Mormon] by the gift and power of God . . . ("Last Days of Oliver Cowdery," *Deseret News*, 13 Apr. 1859, p. 48)

Scripture

Two days after the arrival of Mr. [Oliver] Cowdery (being the 7th of April) I commenced to translate the Book of Mormon, and he began to write for me. (Joseph Smith - History 1: 67)

Visual Aid:
GAPK # 401
The Prophet Joseph Smith

Scripture:

. . . His name was John, the same that is called John the Baptist in the New Testament, and that he acted under the direction of Peter, James, and John, who held the keys of the Priesthood of Melchizedek, which priesthood, he said would in due time be conferred upon us.
(Joseph Smith—History 1:72)

Visual Aid:
GAPK # 408
Melchizedek Priesthood
Restoration

Priesthood authority was restored by heavenly messengers.

Joseph Smith did many great things to help restore the gospel. Many heavenly messengers visited him with information and authority to complete the tasks Heavenly Father wanted him to do.

A very important part of organizing Christ's church as it was in Jesus' day was restoring the priesthood. Joseph explained that the priesthood is the authority from God to act in his name *and* it is also the actual power to do the work.

In 1823, the angel Moroni promised Joseph that the priesthood would be revealed by a resurrected being named Elijah. But first came John the Baptist, who conferred the Aaronic Priesthood on Joseph and Oliver Cowdery. Next came the apostles Peter, James and John who conferred the Melchizedek Priesthood.

Joseph taught that the priesthood is eternal and has been with God from eternity. It is necessary to baptize, to confer the gift of the Holy Ghost, and to administer the sacrament with the proper authority.

We are blessed with living prophets in Jesus Christ's restored church.

Because of Joseph Smith's obedience to Heavenly Father to restore the true church, we once again have a living prophet on the earth.

What is a living prophet? He may be young or old. What he looks like isn't important. He doesn't have to go to college or take special classes. He may be rich or poor. What is it, then, that makes a man a prophet?

Only one thing, God must choose him! This is entirely different than for man to choose a prophet. The Savior, speaking to his apostles, said, "Ye have not chosen me, but I have chosen you, and ordained you, that ye should go and bring forth fruit . . . " (John 15:16.)

A prophet, then, is the authorized representative of the Lord. The world may not recognize him, but we know that God speaks through him. A prophet is a teacher. He receives revelations from the Lord. These may be new truths or truths already received.

Joseph Smith was the first prophet of our times and Gordon B. Hinckley is the true and living prophet today.

Scripture

What I the Lord have spoken, I have spoken, and I excuse not myself; and though the heavens and the earth pass away, my word shall not pass away, but shall all be fulfilled, whether by mine own voice or by the voice of my servants, it is the same. (D&C 1:38)

Visual Aid:
GAPK # 400 - Joseph Smith
GAPK # 520 - Gordon B. Hinckley

Chapter 6:

I will follow Heavenly Father's plan for me in faith

Scripture:

Yea, and how is it that ye have forgotten that the Lord is able to do all things according to his will, for the children of men, if it so be that they exercise faith in him? Wherefore, let us be faithful to him.
(1 Nephi 7:12)

Visual Aid:
GAPK # 613
Administering to the Sick

Faith in Jesus Christ is the first principle of the gospel.

In the Articles of Faith, we say, "We believe that the first principles and ordinances of the gospel are first, Faith in the Lord Jesus Christ."

But how do you explain what faith is to someone who does not understand? Here are some ideas to share.

Faith is believing in things that are not seen but that are true. To have faith in Jesus Christ means that even though I cannot see Him, I believe He lives and I trust and obey Him. I can make my faith stronger by learning more about the the Savior. When I attend Primary and listen to my teacher, when I listen to my parents in Family Home Evening, when I hear testimonies or read my scriptures, my faith in Jesus increases.

Faith means that I really believe Heavenly Father and Jesus Christ are in charge of this world. Faith means I believe Heavenly Father and the Savior know me and love me, and know what is best for me. If I obey the commandments, work hard, and trust in their plan, everything will always be okay, one way or another.

I learn about Jesus Christ as I read the scriptures and my faith increases.

Do you believe the sun is hot? How do you know it is? Did you play in the sunshine one day with a friend and get a sunburn or have to jump in the swimming pool to cool off? You might say you "experienced" the sun. You know about it because you felt it, played in it, tried it out.

If you want to learn about Jesus, you have to go to the place where you can "experience" him, too—just like sunshine. The best place to learn about the Savior is in the scriptures.

Here are some ways to read scriptures you might enjoy:

1. Read one or more verses of scripture every day.
2. Read scriptures out loud with your family.
3. Read scripture stories from *The Friend* magazine.
4. After hearing a scripture story in church, find it in your scriptures at home and read it, or have someone read it to you.

The more you read about the Savior, the stronger your faith will grow.

Scripture

But because of the faith of men he has shown himself unto the world, and glorified the name of the Father, and prepared a way that thereby others might be partakers of the heavenly gift, that they might hope for those things which they have not seen.
(Ether 12:8)

Visual Aid:
GAPK # 617
Search the Scriptures

33

My faith grows when I am obedient to the commandments.

When Jesus lived on earth, He blessed and healed little children. He wanted them to be near Him and talk with Him. When He prayed for the Nephite children, the angels of heaven came down and surrounded them. When someone loves us that much, we want to love them right back. We can show our love for the Lord by keeping the commandments. And the more we keep the commandments, the more our faith in the Savior grows. Jesus will provide a way for us to keep the commandments if we have a little faith and just try.

Daniel was a young man who obeyed the Lord, even though he lived in a land where very few people believed the Lord was real. One day some evil men through Daniel in a pit with lions. But Daniel had faith. He knew because he had kept the commandments that the Lord would help him. He was right. The Lord sent an angel and no hungry lion even scratched Daniel. The more I am obedient and show my love to the Lord, the more he will answer my prayers and help me when I call upon Him.

Visual Aid:
GAPK # 117
Daniel in the Lion's Den

Heavenly Father blesses me when I'm faithful.

As a young man, the prophet, Gordon B. Hinckley, often worked for the railroad. It helped him understand how the light of faith can guide us through dark times when we are discouraged or sad, like a train going through a tunnel with only a headlight to show the way.

When President Hinckley worked for the railroad, he sometimes rode the train that hurtled through narrow mountain passes at night. It had a steam engine— very big, fast, and dangerous. Sometimes it was also scary. President Hinckley wondered how a train engineers\ could make such long dangerous journeys at night. Then the Spirit told him it was not *one* long journey, but rather a lot of *short* journeys. The engine had a powerful headlight that made the way bright for a short distance. The engineer saw only that distance, but that was enough.

"And so it is with us. We take one step at a time. In doing so we reach toward the unknown, but faith lights the way. If we will cultivate that faith, we shall never walk in darkness." (*The Friend*, August 2003, 2)

Scripture

"That which is of God is light; and he that receiveth light, and continueth in God, receiveth more light; and that light groweth brighter and brighter until the perfect day."
(D&C 50:23-24)

Visual Aid:
GAPK # 520
Gordon B. Hinckley

35

Chapter 7:

I follow Heavenly Father's plan by repenting and being baptized

Scripture:

Now I say unto you that ye must repent, and be born again . . . Yea, come and go forth, and show unto your god that ye are willing to repent of your sins and enter into a covenant with him to keep his commandments, and witness it unto him this day by going into the waters of baptism.
(Alma 7:14-16)

Visual Aid:
GAPK # 309
Alma Baptizes in the Water of Mormon

I will choose the right. I know I can repent when I make a mistake.

Repentance means to stop doing what is wrong and begin doing what is right. The Savior wants you to turn away from wrong and remember He gave His life to pay for your sins.

When you disobey, or hurt others, the Holy Ghost cannot be with you. You may feel sad, guilty, lonely, or afraid. To change these feelings, pray to Heavenly Father and Jesus Christ for help. This is called repentance.

Repentance begins in your thoughts and heart. When you know what you did was wrong, do not make excuses or blame someone else. Tell Heavenly Father what you have done and how you feel. Tell Him you love Him and ask for His help. Promise Heavenly Father that you will try, with all your heart, to do what is right from now on.

Heavenly Father knows you will need to repent many times in your life. As you do, you will feel closer to to Him and the Savior. Jesus promised that if you repent, He will bless you and remember your wrongs no more. (See Helaman. 13:11; D&C 58:42.)

Jesus Christ was baptized when He lived on the earth. When I am baptized, I am following the example of Jesus.

Jesus gave us baptism along time ago—first to Adam and Eve and then to all who have lived ever since. Jesus himself was baptized by John the Baptist to set an example.

Immersion is the only true way to be baptized, and it has a real meaning. It represents the burial and resurrection of Christ. As he was buried in the tomb, so we are buried in the water. As Jesus came out of the tomb to a new life as a resurrected person, so *we* come out of the water at baptism to a new way of living on earth—serving the Lord and keeping his commandments.

Our immersion is to help us remember the burial and resurrection of Christ. This is one reason baptism is so important. It will always remind us that Christ died and was resurrected. And when we take the sacrament, we can remember again that we promised at baptism to repent and try every day to be more like the Savior.

Scripture

And it came to pass in those days, that Jesus came from Nazareth of Galilee, and was baptized of John in Jordan.
(Mark 1:9)

Visual Aid:
GAPK # 208
John the Baptist Baptizing Jesus

When I am baptized, I covenant with Heavenly Father to remember Jesus and keep His commandments.

Scripture:

And now, because of the covenant which ye have made ye shall be called the children of Christ, his sons, and his daughters. (Mosiah 5:7)

Visual Aid:

GAPK # 608
Christ and Children From Around the World

If you want to be happy and feel blessed, keep the covenant you made when you were baptized. A covenant is a special promise made by two people, you and Heavenly Father.

When you are baptized you promise to keep the commandments and to remember Jesus and try to be like him. Heavenly Father promises in return that you will always have his Spirit (the Holy Spirit) to be with you.

Since we all make mistakes, the Holy Ghost will prompt you to repent. If you follow the promptings of the Holy Ghost, you can be protected from danger. Sometimes the Holy Spirit may come and bring comfort or inspiration. All of these things are great blessings to receive if you keep your part of the promise, or covenant, you made at baptism—to remember Jesus and try every day to be a little more like Him.

When I partake of the sacrament worthily, I remember and renew my baptismal covenant.

Jesus Christ taught his disciples that when they took the sacrament every Sabbath day, they were renewing their baptismal covenants. They promised all over again to always remember the Savior, to take His name upon them, and to keep His commandments.

Today, we take the sacrament just as Jesus taught his apostles. Each Sunday we can renew our covenants and think about our Savior while the sacrament is being blessed and passed. During this special time, we should show Heavenly Father how grateful we are for all He has done for us by being reverent.

Partaking of the sacrament is a time to think quietly about the good things you have been blessed with and a time to promise to keep the commandments and think of the Savior more often, in all you do and all you say. The Lord promises if you will take the sacrament worthily, he will bless you with peace in your heart and in your mind.

Scripture

When they had partaken of it, Jesus said, "And this shall ye always do . . . ; and ye shall do it in remembrance of my blood, which I have shed for you, that ye may witness unto the Father that ye do always remember me. And if ye do always remember me ye shall have my Spirit to be with you."
(3 Ne. 18:11)

Visual Aid:
GAPK # 604
Passing the Sacrament

Chapter 8:

The Holy Ghost is a gift from Heavenly Father

Scripture:

And by the power of the Holy Ghost ye may know the truth of all things. (Moroni 10:5)

Visual Aid:
GAPK # 400
Joseph Smith

The Holy Ghost is the third member of the Godhead and testifies of Jesus.

When Joseph Smith was fourteen, he was reading his scriptures, as his mom and dad had taught him to do. He had some questions and he was confused. There were so many churches in his town, and he wanted to make sure he went to the right church, the church that would make Heavenly Father happy with him.

He read a scripture, John 1:5, that says if any man lacks wisdom, let him ask of God. Joseph said that no scripture had ever had such a powerful feeling over his heart like this one did. So he went out to a special place and prayed for knowledge.

The strong power that entered Joseph's heart was brought by the Holy Spirit. The Holy Spirit, or Holy Ghost, can tell any of us what is right or wrong, bring us comfort when we feel sad, or protect us by making us feel we need to change where we're walking or to go home when danger is near. But in order to feel or hear the still small voice, we must try very hard to keep the commandments, do what is right, and try to be like Jesus.

I receive the gift of the Holy Ghost by the laying on of hands.

During our lives, we sometimes have to face hard choices or hidden dangers. President James E. Faust tells us how we can receive personal revelation that will lead us to strength and safety.

"The right to enjoy the marvelous gifts of the Holy Ghost is conferred upon every member of the Church soon after baptism . . . This powerful gift entitles the leaders and all worthy members of the Church to enjoy the gifts of the Holy Ghost, a member of the Godhead whose function is to inspire, reveal, and teach all things." (*The Friend, June 2002, 2*)

Once the gift of the Holy Ghost is given by the laying on of hands by someone with the Melchizedek priesthood, a person can receive personal inspiration, or special feelings, for small decisions or big ones. Heavenly Father loves us so much, He has given us the chance to have the Holy Spirit with us if we keep trying to do what is good and live worthy to feel the promptings and whispers of the still small voice.

Scripture

But when the Comforter is come, whom I will send unto you from the Father, even the Spirit of truth, *which proceedeth from the Father, he shall testify of me.*
(*John 15:26*)

Visual Aid:
GAPK # 602
The Gift of the Holy Ghost

45

I will remember my baptismal covenant and listen to the Holy Ghost.

Scripture:

And I was led by the Spirit, not knowing beforehand the things which I should do.
(1 Nephi 4:6)

The Savior said baptism is like being reborn. You probably don't remember the day you were born, but it's not hard to remember your baptism—your second birth.

When you are baptized you are clean from head to toe and then you can receive the companionship of the Savior through the gift of the Holy Ghost. He will be with each baptized person if they strive to do what is right.

Now, you are a member of Christ's church and having received the gift of the Holy Ghost, you will have the spiritual power to become holy. The Holy Ghost will help you remember you were born a son or daughter of a Heavenly King, our Heavenly Father. By being baptized, you have been promised the blessings of royalty.

If you keep your baptismal covenants—to try always to remember Jesus and keep his commandments—you will have the Holy Ghost with you all the time. When you say your prayers, ask Heavenly Father to prepare you to take the sacrament so that the power of your baptism will be with you all week.

Visual Aid:
GAPK # 238
The Second Coming

I can feel the influence of the Holy Ghost. My life is blessed when I follow His promptings.

Mary Fielding married Hyrum Smith, the brother of the Prophet Joseph. Hyrum's first wife had died and left five small children. Mary helped take care of them. Later, two more children came—Martha Ann and Joseph F. Smith, who would become the sixth President of the Church. When Hyrum and Joseph Smith were killed, Mary had to take care of seven children all by herself.

Mary and her children traveled to Nauvoo. Then they journeyed to St. Joseph, Missouri, to get some supplies. Joseph F. and his uncle Joseph Fielding went with Mary to help. One morning they woke up to find their oxen missing. Joseph and his uncle searched all morning, but returned to camp sad without the oxen. They found Mary kneeling in prayer, asking the Lord to help them recover their lost team. She then started toward the river and soon found the oxen by a clump of willows. The Holy Ghost had told her where to find the lost team. She listened to the promptings and her family was blessed.

Scripture

Verily, verily, I say unto thee, blessed art thou for what thou hast done; for thou hast inquired of me, and behold, as often as thou hast inquired thou hast received instruction of my Spirit.
(D&C 6:14)

Visual Aid:
GAPK # 412
Mary Fielding and Joseph F. Smith Crossing the Plains

Chapter 9:
I follow Heavenly Father's plan when I choose the right

Scripture:

Counsel with the Lord in all thy doings, and he will direct thee for good; yea, when thou liest down at night lie down unto the Lord, that he may watch over you in your sleep; and when thou risest in the morning let thy heart be full of thanks unto God; and if ye do these things, ye shall be lifted up at the last day.
(Alma 37:37)

Visual Aid:
GAPK # 605
Young Boy Praying

As I pray and study the scriptures, I learn what Heavenly Father wants me to do.

Can you remember the last time you received an answer to your prayers? Maybe you were sick and Heavenly Father told you to rest and do what your mother told you (drink lots of water!) Perhaps someone hurt your feelings and you went to your scriptures to find out about forgiveness by reading about Joseph of Egypt.

We can pray to Heavenly Father anytime, anywhere. He will always hear our prayers. He has given us the scriptures to learn from. There are many stories and examples of people who had hard decisions to make. There might be sick family members or folks who did not know what to do or where to go. Then they prayed and Heavenly Father answered them through the still small voice of the Holy Spirit, who spoke to their minds or gave them a warm feeling in their heart.

When we read the scriptures and pray about what we've read, Heavenly Father will help us find the way.

I choose the right when I pay tithing gladly.

The Lord told Joseph Smith that the Saints should pay tithing. The Prophet prayed to Heavenly Father to find out how much tithing was required of them and the Lord revealed that the Saints should pay one-tenth of all their income for tithing.

If a person earns ten cents, one penny is paid for tithing. And if a person earns one hundred dollars, ten dollars is for tithing. In the early days of the church, the Saints could also pay tithing "in kind" on the crops they harvested or the livestock they raised by giving a tenth of their crops or livestock to the bishop.

Tithing money is used in many ways: to help needy members of the Church obtain food and clothing, to build temples and meetinghouses, or to help with missionary work. Tithing is given to the bishop or branch president, and he sends the tithing to Church headquarters, where it is decided how the tithing will be used.

Heavenly Father promised wonderful blessings to those who pay their tithing. If I pay my tithing gladly, I will be helping and serving others; I will feel happy inside.

Scripture

Bring ye all the tithes into the storehouse, that there may be meat in mine house, and prove me now herewith, saith the Lord of hosts, if I will not open you the windows of heaven, and pour you out a blessing, that there shall not be room enough to receive it. (Malachi 3:10)

Visual Aid:
GAPK # 503
Salt Lake Tabernacle

I will be honest with Heavenly Father, others, and myself.

Scripture:

We believe in being honest, true, chaste, benevolent, virtuous, and in doing good to all men.
(The Articles of Faith;13)

Visual Aid:
GAPK # 618
The Articles of Faith

Honesty and the ability to be trusted are important ways for people to know us. Being honest is so important that our Father in Heaven included it in the Ten Commandments: "Thou shalt not steal" and, "Thou shalt not bear false witness (lie)."

There are other ways of stealing besides taking money or things that do not belong to us. Not doing a job right or on time that we are being paid for is stealing time and money from the person paying us. If you tell someone you will do a thing you have been asked to do, and then don't do it, you are being dishonest and teaching others that you cannot be trusted. Honesty means keeping your word and living up to any agreement you make.

Paying your tithing is also a way to show you are honest. The Bible says that people who do not pay tithing are robbing God, for everything belongs to Him. If I want to be a friend to Jesus and show my love for Heavenly Father, I will always try to do what I promise, pay an honest tithe, and pay for things I want to own.

I will use the names of Heavenly Father and Jesus Christ reverently. I will not swear or use crude words.

As members of Christ's church, we know it is important to set a good example. Because we know what is right and wrong, we have more responsibility to be careful with the words we choose to use when we speak. Here is an example from Prophet Spencer W. Kimball.

After an operation, a young man was wheeling President Kimball back to his hospital room. The strong medicine used during the operation made the prophet barely conscious. Then the young man got angry at something. He swore, using the Lord's name. President Kimball tried hard to speak, although his throat hurt very badly. He said to the young man, "Please . . . don't say that. I love the Savior . . . more than anything in this world. Please." At first, the young man was silent. Then he apologized. The young man said, "I shouldn't have said that. I'm sorry."

Whenever we use the right words and set a good example, we get a warm feeling inside. This is the Holy Spirit telling us that Heavenly Father is pleased.

Scripture

Thou shalt not take the name of the Lord in vain; for the Lord will not hold him guiltless that taketh his name in vain.
(Exodus 20:7)

Visual Aid:
GAPK # 517
Spencer W. Kimball

Chapter 10:

I follow Heavenly Father's plan when I choose the right

I will do things on the Sabbath
that help me feel close to Heavenly Father
and Jesus Christ.

Scripture:

Choose you this day whom ye will serve; . . . but as for me and my house, we will serve the Lord."
(Joshua 24:15)

One of the ten commandments says we should rest and not do any kind of work on the Sabbath day. Even Heavenly Father rested after six days of work. Why is it so important to keep the Sabbath day holy, that even a commandment was made?

The scriptures say the Sabbath was made for man and not man for the Sabbath (Mark 2:27). This means Heavenly Father knew it was so important for our minds and bodies to rest, that he gave us a special day just for that reason. Sterling W. Sills said, "After we have laid aside the cares that have concerned us during the other six days, we go to the house of prayer and let our minds reach up and try to comprehend the things of God."

Resting doesn't mean just taking a nap. It also means reading—*The Friend* or the scriptures, visiting people who are sick or visiting friends and relatives. We can write letters, sing Church hymns and plan Family Home Evenings.

Visual Aid:
GAPK #604
Passing the Sacrament

I will keep my mind and body sacred and pure, and not partake of things that are harmful to me.

As members of Christ's church, we know it is important to keep the Word of Wisdom and treat our bodies as temples. Treating our bodies with respect has always been a part of the gospel plan.

In the Bible we learn about Daniel, who was captured by Babylonians with three of his friends. The king wanted them to eat his best food and wine, but Daniel refused, saying these kinds of food were not good for them. The servant was afraid that the other young men eating the king's food would look healthier. Daniel pleaded with the servant to allow him and his friends to eat vegetables and drink water for ten days and then decide whether the four of them looked healthy or not. The servant agreed. Ten days passed and the servant saw that Daniel and his friends looked healthier than the other youth. The Lord blessed Daniel and the king respected them for their clear minds and devoted ways.

Scripture

Know ye not that ye are the temple of God, and that the Spirit of God dwelleth in you? If any man defile the temple of God, him shall God destroy; for the temple of God is holy, which temple ye are.
(1 Corinthians 3:16-17))

Visual Aid:
GAPK # 114
Daniel Refusing the King's meat and Wine

I will only read and watch things that are pleasing to Heavenly Father.

Your eyes and ears send messages to your mind that become memories. Sometimes a bad thought or word can come into your head very quickly, all by itself. TV, videos, and books can be very good tools to learn and be entertained by, but they can also put bad words and images in your mind that are hard to get rid of. The thirteenth Article of Faith helps us know what to choose: "If there is anything virtuous, lovely, or of good report or praiseworthy, we seek after these things."

When a bad thought or word comes into your mind it is not a good feeling, because the Holy Spirit cannot stay with you. Here are some tools to use when this happens.

Only one thought at a time can be in your mind, so when a bad thought or word comes, sing a Primary song or hymn. Say your blessings out loud or think of the beautiful things that Heavenly Father and Jesus have created for you. As you watch a video or read a book, think how you would feel if Jesus was sitting with you. Would you still want to watch or read it? Let the Holy Spirit guide.

I will seek good friends and treat others kindly.

Our Savior is often called the God of Love. One reason for this is because when He came to earth He told people that they should love one another. If someone is unkind to you, He said to pray for them. If someone needs to borrow your coat, give them your hat, too. The Law of Moses said, "An eye for an eye, a tooth for a tooth." But Jesus said love those who despitefully use you and pray for your enemies. People were amazed by this.

The Prophet Joseph Smith taught people about God's love by his example. He was especially kind to children. One time, a girl named Margarette and her brother were walking to school on a muddy road. They got stuck in the mud and could not get out. The harder they tried to get out, the deeper they went into the mud. They became frightened and started to cry.

Joseph saw the children as he was coming from his store. He pulled them out of the mud, put them on dry ground and cleaned the mud from their shoes with his own handkerchief. Like Jesus, Joseph loved children.

Scripture

A new commandment I give unto you, that ye love one another; as I have loved you, that ye also love one another. By this shall men know that ye are my disciples, if ye have love one to another.
(John 13:34-35)

Visual Aid:
GAPK # 420
The Prophet Joseph Loved Children

Chapter 11:

I can share the gospel so that others can follow Heavenly Father's plan

I share the gospel so others can follow Heavenly Father's plan.

Scripture:

Let your light so shine before men, that they may see your good works, and glorify your Father which is in heaven.
(Matthew 5:16)

Do you know what it is like when a rain storm shuts off the electricity and everything is dark? It can be a little scary. A light, even a little light, like a flashlight, makes a big difference.

Jesus Christ said we are to be "the light of the world." He said don't light candles and put them under baskets. Being a light to someone means to show the way by the way you act, by being a good example. When you are a good example, then you show people that you love Heavenly Father and He is so important to you that you will even do what is right when others around you do not.

There are many people in the world that do not know about Heavenly Father or Jesus. When you dress modestly, use good language, act kindly, help others, keep the Word of Wisdom, and honor the Sabbath day, you are acting like a light, a candle or a flashlight, to show others the way to the gospel. Let your light so shine.

Visual Aid:
GAPK # 615
Serving One Another

I share the gospel as I serve others.

George Albert Smith was the president and prophet of the Church for six years, just as World War II ended. He was well-loved by members of the Church and non-members, too. He had a personal creed, or motto, that he lived by: "I would be a friend to the friendless and find joy in ministering to the needs of the poor."

After World War II was over, President Smith sent train-carloads of supplies to members of the Church in Europe where most of the war's fighting took place. Then he sent tons of wheat to nonmembers in Greece who were suffering from starvation. He remembered what it was to be hungry when he was a child, so he did all he could to help others. He could not rest while he knew of suffering. He said, "I would visit the sick and afflicted and inspire in them a faith to be healed." He also visited hospitals whenever he could. He helped a woman on a train that was a stranger and made sure she and her children made their long journey safely. He knew that to love the Lord was to serve His fellowman.

Scripture

And behold, I tell you these things that ye may learn wisdom; that ye may learn that when ye are in the service of your fellow beings ye are only in the service of your God.
(Mosiah 2:17)

Visual Aid:
GAPK # 513
George Albert Smith

I share the gospel as I bear my testimony.

Ye are blessed, for the testimony which ye have borne is recorded in heaven.
(D&C 62:3)

To have a testimony means to stand as a witness when you know that something is true. To *bear* a testimony means to carry it with you and show that you believe the gospel is true by the way you behave and how you dress and speak. John Taylor, third president of the church traveled to Kirtland, Ohio to meet the Prophet Joseph Smith. When he shook hands with the Prophet, he felt "a charge like an electric shock" and gained a testimony right then that Joseph was a prophet of God.

Another time, at Sunday meetings some people were criticizing the Prophet when he wasn't there. Although just a new member, John Taylor asked for permission to speak at the meeting and he bore testimony of the Prophet Joseph Smith. It made people stop saying unkind things about the Prophet very quickly.

When Joseph Smith was falsely accused and arrested, John Taylor went to jail with him and his brother Hyrum. He was shot several times but later said, "I know we are not alone! God is with us and He will continue with us from this time henceforth and forever."

Visual Aid:
GAPK # 508
John Taylor

I want to be a missionary.

Every member of the Church who has a testimony can be a missionary and share the gospel with non-member friends and neighbors.

We can be missionaries by showing love to others. You can be a friend to someone who is new to your school or invite your neighbor to come to primary with you. When you use good manners, people can feel the love of the Savior through your behavior and might even start to ask questions about the Church.

We are missionaries when we share our testimony that Heavenly Father loves *all* His children. Heavenly Father wants us to talk about the Prophet Joseph Smith, President Hinckley, the Book of Mormon, or being a forever family. The Holy Spirit can tell you when someone is ready to hear about the gospel, if you keep the commandments and pray to know what Father wants you to do.

David O. McKay, one of the Presidents of the Church said, "Every member a missionary." When we are good examples, people will see how happy we are and want to know more about the Church.

Scripture

For I am not ashamed of the gospel of Christ: for it is the power of God unto salvation to every one that believeth.
(Rom. 1:16)

Visual Aid:
GAPK # 612
Missionaries Teach the Gospel of Jesus Christ

Chapter 12:

Heavenly Father's plan brings us many blessings

I am grateful for Heavenly Father's plan.

Scripture:

Adam fell that men might be; and men are, that they might have joy.
(2 Nephi 2:25)

Visual Aid:
GAPK # 119
Adam and Eve Teach Their Children

The plan of salvation is also called "the great plan of happiness" (Alma 42:8). This is because we know without this wonderful plan from our Heavenly Father and our Savior that we would never have a chance to learn and grow and choose. We would be like a flower that never blooms or a caterpillar that never turns into a butterfly.

As a member of the Church we learn the answer to questions such as—where did we come from? Why are we here? and, what happens to us when we die? These things are answered through the gospel of Jesus Christ and modern-day revelation from a living prophet and other servants of the Lord. Heavenly Father's great plan is a map of to guide us through this earth life.

Because we are here on earth to work to prove our trust in God and our willingness to obey, we have a unique perspective and inspired values to guide our decisions. To realize a fulness of joy, we can prove we will keep the commandments of God even though we have no memory of what took place before our birth.

I am grateful for the Prophet Joseph Smith.

This year we celebrate the 200th anniversary of the birth of Joseph Smith. He sealed his testimony of the Book of Mormon and the restoration of the gospel with his blood when he was killed by a mob in June 1844.

It is wonderful to remember the example of the Prophet Joseph and all his sacrifices so we can have the restored gospel and modern-day revelation on the earth today. He was made fun of for saying what was true, that Heavenly Father and Jesus Christ live. He was arrested and jailed many times, and tarred and feathered, but he kept teaching the gospel, organizing the Church, translating the Book of Mormon, and telling the truth.

Joseph Smith also played games with children, laughed with his friends, wrote letters to his wife Emma and his children, helped people who were sick, and worked hard to support his family. He repented of his sins and often said he was not perfect, but every day he prayed very hard and did the things Heavenly Father instructed him to do. "He lived great and he died great in the eyes of God and his people." (John Taylor)

Scripture

Joseph Smith, the Prophet and Seer of the Lord, has done more, save Jesus only, for the salvation of men in this world, than any other man that ever lived in it.
(D&C135:3)

Visual Aid:
GAPK # 401
The Prophet Joseph Smith

I am grateful for the birth of the Savior.

From the time of Adam, men looked forward to the birth of Jesus Christ, our Savior. The prophets taught that Jesus Christ would come to save all of us from death. They also taught that through Jesus Christ's Atonement, everyone could be forgiven of their sins. Many prophets knew of the birth of the Savior long before it happened and wrote about it in the scriptures.

Isaiah, a prophet of the Old Testament, spoke of the Savior's birth. Lehi from the Book of Mormon, prophesied and his son Nephi recorded, "Six hundred years from the time that my father left Jerusalem, a prophet would the Lord God raise up among the Jews—even a Messiah, or, in other words, a Savior of the world" (1 Ne. 10:4). Samuel the Lamanite also prophesied these things.

When the Savior was born, the prophecies were fulfilled. An angel appeared to shepherds watching their flocks and said, "Fear not: for, behold, I bring you good tidings of great joy, which shall be to all people" (Luke 2:10).

In heaven we were all watching and we shouted for joy because our Savior was born!

I am grateful for the gift of eternal life.

The Prophet Joseph Smith said, "Here, then, is eternal life—to know the only wise and true God."

It is wonderful to live in a time when we have all we need to help us truly know what is right and wrong, which church is true, and who to believe. Because of the plan of salvation—the plan of happiness, we know if we try to do our best, keep learning and repenting of our mistakes, and practice living the gospel every day, we can go back to our heavenly home.

Because the Savior was resurrected, we know that everyone that comes to earth will also be resurrected. We also know that if we keep the covenants we make at baptism, trying to be like Jesus, that we will also have eternal life. Each of us is on the path toward our eternal home. When we are lonely, sad, or confused, we can pray and turn to God. The gift of this life is our one chance to repent and have our sins erased. Our only chance to find peace and happiness on earth and eternal life in the world to come, is to follow the Savior and keep the commandments. How wonderful it is to have all of the gospel again on the earth.

Scripture

Behold, I stand at the door, and knock: if any man hear my voice, and open the door, I will come in to him.
(Revelation 3:20)

Visual Aid:
GAPK # 237
Jesus at the Door

Other volumes in the
Tiny Talks series:

Volume 1:
The Temple

Volume 2:
The Savior

Volume 3:
*The Church of
Jesus Christ*

Volume 4:
The Family

About the author

Janet Bernice was raised in Prescott, Arizona and has been writing since she was eight years old, inspired by her grandmother Bernice Insley, the author of *Indian Folklore* and the past director of the Smoki Museum with her husband Russell Insley.

She is the mother of five children and currently, the grandmother to seven—Preston, Chase, Carter, Brynn, Dorothy, Jacob, and Damian. One of her greatest joys is sharing her love of books with all of them by reading to them every chance she gets.

A 1995—graduate of the University of Utah with a bachelor's degree in English and Creative Writing, Janet has written for the Bountiful *Clipper*, *Ancestry Magazine* and contributed to *The Ensign*. She has also written for television and co-written screenplays while working in the film industry in Los Angeles.

A grateful convert to the Church for thirty-two years, Janet serves wherever she is asked in the Springville, Utah Third Ward and especially loves visiting teaching.

She is the current Executive Editor for Cedarfort, Inc. in Springville, Utah.

The Bob Bonham Family

About the illustrator

Bob Bonham studied cartoon animation at Orange Coast College of California and graduated from El Camino College in Los Angeles County, California with an emphasis in Illustration and Graphic Design.

He grew up in Redondo Beach, California where he learned to play guitar and has since played in various performance and recording venues. He now lives in Highland, Utah with his eternal companion and best friend, Mary. They have been blessed with three daughters, one son-in-law, two grandsons, a dog, a cat, and a parakeet.

Bob currently works as a freelance artist and also teaches guitar. He illustrated Cedar Fort's first children's board book, *Book of Mormon Numbers*.

9 26575 78154 3